THE STORY OF
THE HIGHWAY ACROSS GLACIER NATIONAL PARK
GOING-TO-THE-SUN

WORDS BY ROSE HOUK WITH PHOTOGRAPHY BY PAT O'HARA & DANNY ON
DESIGNED BY MCQUISTON & DAUGHTER

Published by Woodlands Press, Del Mar, A Division of Robert White & Associates
in conjunction with Glacier Natural History Association

This book is dedicated to the farsighted and courageous people
who planned and built Going-to-the-Sun Highway and to the personnel
of Waterton/Glacier International Peace Park for their untiring
stewardship of an irreplaceable resource.

A Dotted Line on the Map

Morton J. Elrod, in 1924, advised travelers to Glacier National Park of rules they should observe while on park roads: "Automobiles in motion must be not less than fifty yards apart, except when passing. Gears must be kept enmeshed except when changing. Speed is 12 miles on grades, 20 miles on open stretches. Horns must be sounded on curves. . . . Muffler cutouts must be closed passing horses, hotels, camps, or checking station." Elrod further cautioned that a leaner gasoline mixture was demanded by the park's high altitudes, and that drivers should shift one gear lower on grades. These same long hills might lead to an overheated engine, "which may become serious unless care is used."

At the time of Elrod's writing, the Transmountain Highway, later named Going-to-the-Sun Road, was only a dotted line on a map. Major construction that would join the east side of Glacier National Park to its west side, across the Continental Divide, was only beginning. But Americans' infatuation with the automobile was in the heat of its youth, and the inevitable marriage of cars and roads did not bypass even this most remote region. One measure of the lure that access lent to the park is seen in number of visits: in 1925 some 40,000 people visited the park; by 1936, after Going-to-the-Sun Road had been open to through traffic for two years, that number had risen dramatically, to 210,000, despite the effects of the Great Depression.

The road revealed a portion of the most romantic western landscape the nation had to offer. Not only the wealthy leisure class, but the burgeoning middle class as well could follow the route through stately expanses of virgin forest, past deep, clear, glacier-carved lakes, alongside vertigo-inspiring cliffs, and through luxuriant meadows of delicate alpine flowers. At Logan Pass, 6,646 feet above sea level, travelers could emerge from their tin lizzies and inhale the crisp mountain air atop the "Crown of the Continent." It would most certainly be a trip to write home about.

Unavoidably, as they kept a close eye on the gears and the engine temperature, tourists would be impressed with the engineering feat that Going-to-the-Sun Road represented. Indeed, it was a "modern automobile highway" of "front rank," according to the Bureau of Public Roads. Applying their imaginations, visitors could begin to appreciate the hazards

R oughing it—1920s style. No longer restricted to relatively expensive trains or tours, Americans could see their country from their own cars. They had only to pitch a tent, spread some blankets, set out the pots and pans, and Glacier National Park was theirs to explore. Others chose to see the park from buses run by a private company. The group below heads across the foot of St. Mary Lake towards Logan Pass. Cloth tops on the buses were rolled back during fair weather for a better view.

involved in construction—blasting rock out of sheer cliffs, bridging rushing streams, working in inclement weather. It was truly a dizzying prospect.

Planning and building the 52 miles of road had taken nearly twenty years and $3 million, but the project's boosters were farsighted individuals who never took no for an answer, and who never doubted that the job could be accomplished. At the time that Glacier attained parkhood, on May 11, 1910, the main option open to visitors was to see the park from the back of a horse. A few wagon roads existed, but none spanned the mountains from east to west. As soon as the land became a park, however, plans were unfurled to provide access to it. The Great Northern Railway, whose line ran on the park's southern boundary, exerted initiative and energy in those early years, undertaking with its own funds to improve some roads and trails to its Swiss-style chalets and lodges inside the park.

The newly founded National Park Service saw that private enterprise could not bear the total burden of making these "playgrounds" accessible to the public. After much debate over a suitable route, and after several reconnaissance surveys and subsequent resurveys, the Logan Pass route for Going-to-the-Sun Road was selected. With meager appropriations from Congress, contracts were let, crews were hired, and work was begun; twelve years later, in 1933, officials gathered at Logan Pass on a July day to praise the road and its builders. It was an era of engineering marvels, and building the Sun highway merely reinforced the notion that all we had to do was to want something enough, and it could be done.

Black Powder, Crowbars and Determination

The Great Northern Railway saw to it that people knew how to get to Glacier National Park. Through its National Park Line featuring Rocky, the Great Northern Goat as its symbol, the company organized a nationwide advertising campaign to draw people to the park. Trains stopped at Midvale and Belton (now East and West Glacier, respectively), where visitors could rest for the night before mounting a horse or starting out on foot. Ed Dow's buckboard would meet visitors at Belton and take them to the foot of Lake McDonald over what was by 1911 a fairly adequate macadamized road. By one person's account, this was "truly a beautiful trip if you were not thrown from the buckboard by the chuckholes in the road." John Weightman's fringe-topped surreys, or tally-hos, followed the same route as Dow's stages, across a bridge on the Middle Fork of the Flathead River to the lake.

For some time during the park's early days, before automobiles took over the scene, boats were a popular way to get tourists to their destinations. George Snyder's steamboat met the stages and ferried folks to the upper end of Lake McDonald. His was the first power boat to take passengers and freight on the lakes, although one woman found that because of the boiler it was too hot to ride down below, and on topside sparks burned holes in her clothes. Snyder's competition came in the form of a gas-powered craft operated by Frank Kelly, and other boats plied the waters of St. Mary Lake.

For a long time, though, Glacier was best known as a saddle horse park, with some 700 miles of trail at equestrians' disposal. The Park Saddle Horse Company was most successful: in its peak year it took nearly ten thousand visitors on its thousand horses, under the Bar X Six brand, to see the park. Until Going-to-the-Sun Road was completed, this was the preferred way to see Glacier's wonders.

Motorized vehicles did try to negotiate those thoroughfares that existed in the early part of the century. The Glacier Park Transportation Company, backed by the White Motor Company, was given the sole permit to operate the passenger and freight

Stumps of cedars and hemlocks, yet to be cleared, dot the route that was chosen as the first leg of the Trans-mountain Highway. Once improved, this former wagon road—"the worst three miles in Montana"—became passable to adventurous motorists who could then travel to the foot of Lake McDonald, in background.

concession in the park. That was 1914, a dry year, and the company's ten buses and five touring cars had little trouble running. The story was different in 1915. Heavy rains turned the roads to mud, and in some places horses were recruited to pull the buses out of the muck. Passengers arrived at their destinations cross and mud-encrusted. In 1927 Glacier Transport Company took over and three years later had sixty-five red, wooden-topped buses with side curtains to keep out the elements.

In 1911 the complicated transportation picture began to take on a new complexion. Frank Stoop, a Kalispell garage owner, was a passenger in his E-M-F "30," which chugged into Belton and crossed the bridge, proving that what was then loosely referred to as a road was indeed passable to automobiles. But until 1930 the only way to get a car across the Great Divide was to put it on a railroad flatcar and follow it in a passenger coach; Great Northern provided the service for $12.50 per vehicle.

In the same year that Frank Stoop made his landmark auto trip, William R. Logan became the first superintendent of the park. He had started a year earlier as acting superintendent in charge of roads and trails, and his first priority was unmistakable. Logan's most crucial duties upon arrival at Glacier, however, involved fire fighting; it was August 1910, and it had been one of the driest summers on record. All of Logan's attention in those first few months had to be focused on putting out forest fires and protecting property. Not until late in the season, later than he would have liked, could he concentrate fully on road building. He then formed definite plans for carrying through what he felt was

a mandate—to make this "pleasuring ground" accessible to the public. If Congress would provide money that winter, he pledged to do "considerable" construction work the following summer. His goal was to bring a road "from some one of the mountain passes from the east to the west side" of Glacier.

Logan told a U.S. House of Representatives appropriations committee that a road *would* be built from east to west, around Lake McDonald, connecting with the Great Northern. That year Congress saw fit to appropriate the sum of $69,200 for park operations. When Logan returned to the park in April, his first job was to secure rights-of-way from many private landowners for the new road from Belton to Lake McDonald.

At this point only trees and stumps stood in his way. The trees, many of them large hemlocks and red cedars, were cut, the stumps dynamited, and the roadbed graded. Logan reported spending at least $1,000 on dynamite and added that "blowing out the stumps is the hardest part of the work. . . ." The road led through some swampland as well, requiring extensive ditching and draining. When completed in September, what had been termed "the worst and most objurgated three miles in the state of Montana" was glowingly praised by the *Daily Inter Lake* of Kalispell as "a broad, well drained, macadamized highway."

The taste of success whetted appetites. Logan's hard-won 2½ miles would become the western end of the Transmountain Highway that he had promised would be built. It remained, however, for his successors to settle on a route and see the road through to completion.

Major William Logan, *above right,* promised the first road over the mountains. Those who actually built it had to get supplies and equipment to inaccessible sites. *Left,* a Caterpillar hauls bedding into a work camp; *below right,* a horse-drawn "go-devil" drags culvert pipe.

en and machinery struggled against billion-year-old limestone along the Continental Divide. Armed with transits and ropes, surveyors were the pioneers of the Going-to-the-Sun Road. Through pine forests or along precipitous cliffs, they marked the alignment of the roadbed for the blasters who followed. Despite the constant danger of falling rock, the crew at the west side tunnel wore only felt hats and derbies. Once the hand work of cutting the bench was accomplished, heavier vehicles could move to the road site. Highlighted by an early snow, Going-to-the-Sun Mountain looms behind an Autocar dump truck, a Ford truck, and a Lima 101 steam shovel, which handled some of the heavy earth-moving near the east side tunnel below Logan Pass.

Eva Beebe, for one, was a nonbeliever. Wife of park ranger Chauncey E. Beebe, Eva saw the prospective route for Going-to-the-Sun Road from the ground up, and she was not impressed. As Mrs. Beebe recalled, she accompanied her husband and three surveyors from St. Mary Lake to Logan Pass. After lunch, they started walking around the west side of the pass by way of mountain goat trails. The surveyors were thrilled with the sight before them, but Mrs. Beebe did not enjoy it "because I was scared," she said. The ledge on which they were standing was a foot wide, the valley was thousands of feet below, "and the rock I was hanging onto looked like it was loose and ready to fall on me. . . . I finally got down on my hands and knees and crawled." Her feelings could not be soothed by the joking of her husband, who said it was the best goat trail in the park; he urged her to stand up lest she wear out the knees of her breeches. At her pleas, the men yielded and turned back. Once safely in camp, Mrs. Beebe tried unsuccessfully to convince the chief engineer that a road could not be built in such a place. "But he assured me they would and [could] build it for cars to travel."

Mrs. Beebe was not the last person to feel panic at the prospect of building a road through such steep terrain. Years later, in some of the more hair-raising portions of the Going-to-the-Sun construction, workmen refused to perform certain tasks because of the precipitous dropoffs they encountered.

Not until 1921 did continuous effort on Going-to-the-Sun Road begin. In that year Congress appropriated the first "real" money for the road. The $100,000 the park received allowed a contract to be awarded for a 3½-mile section along Lake Mc-Donald, continuing the work Superintendent Logan had started. In the next several years the segment linking the head of the lake to Avalanche Creek was completed, and activity also began on the east side of the mountains along St. Mary Lake.

In 1924, with a flush of more congressional funding, some people began to question the road's planned route over the mountains by way of Logan Creek. Steep grades, almost a dozen creek crossings, and restricted views of the scenery led to the call for a resurvey of the entire route. Telegraphed to begin immediately despite the lateness of the season, Bureau of Public Roads engineer Frank A. Kittredge and a crew of surveyors started work in mid-September. Originally intending to have two parties of about fifteen men each, Kittredge had trouble keeping people on duty. "The daily climb of from 1,200' to 3,000' over cliffs and through brush proved too strenuous for many. Work on the line along the steep mountainside and cliffs proved too hazardous for those not adapted to such work. Working in the rain and sleet was beyond endurance for many more." Finally, they succeeded in staking the road's alignment, but abrupt cliffs and snow and ice prevented staking in a few sections.

The surveyors recommended a route over Logan Pass because it provided a south or west exposure, which meant the road would be in sun and out of the shadows of surrounding peaks—an extremely important consideration in an area that receives at least eight feet of snow a year. The width of the roadway was established as sixteen feet, with an average grade of six percent. This was considered a

An engineer, *below,* puts his trust in little more than a single strand of manila rope. Many road workers found themselves toiling under extreme conditions. *Center,* a workman stands beside a Sullivan compressor, which was probably pulled in by horse-drawn sleds. At the peak of construction on the west side, a sixty-horse pack train shuttled in equipment, tools, fuel, food, and all necessary supplies.

safe grade and one that took advantage of the topography. The road would follow the mountainside at the base of the massive Garden Wall, rising steadily and staying high to put the sun's rays to good use. A sharp switchback, called The Loop, would be necessary, and tunneling would be required at the steepest cliffs. The summit, Logan Pass, would provide a "typical" view of the Continental Divide country: "high mountains, precipitous peaks, cirques, glaciers and cascades," Kittredge reported. A second tunnel would be built 1½ miles east of Logan Pass, from which point the road would continue down through forest to St. Mary Lake.

Hundreds of thousands of cubic yards of rock would have to be excavated, most of it by hand; steam shovels did not appear practical for the project, Kittredge advised. With Logan Pass designated as mile zero, the road project would be handled in two parts—the 12½-mile west side section and 10½ miles on the east side. The west side won top priority; an $870,000 contract was awarded to low bidder Williams and Douglas of Tacoma, Washington, whose bid, contrary to Kittredge's prediction, included use of three power shovels.

In June 1925 the company was at the site, workers were hired, and the west side was under way. To get a shovel to the road cut, access first had to be gained. One of the big expenses for nearly all the Going-to-the-Sun contractors arose in getting equipment and supplies to the sites. Tote roads and trails had to be pioneered before any heavy work could take place. One contractor tried a novel approach; *continued on page 28*

continued on page 28

Avalanche Gorge. *Opposite*, beargrass and Reynolds Mountain.

Glacier lily. *Opposite,* fall foliage and Lake McDonald.

M cDonald Creek in winter. *Opposite,* fog drifting over Logan Pass.

Looking east from Logan Pass. *Opposite,* Avalanche Lake in fall.

Winter ice formations. *Opposite,* Logan Pass with first snow.

he lowered a steam shovel down on its main cable twenty-five feet over a cliff.

At the peak of construction on the west side, a string of sixty pack horses hauled in pipe, rails, fuel, food, and other necessities. Horses could be hired for $.70 a head, with feed furnished. A horse could carry about 150 pounds, so three 50-pound boxes of dynamite made a "well-balanced" load. Special wedge-shaped cans were designed for packing in gasoline, because "any spilled gasoline on a horse's hide soon ruined him for work."

The contractor built six camps along the route, where men could be housed and fed. Workers came from cities, logging camps, and nearby towns; many of them were World War I veterans. Thain White, who was seventeen in 1929, was hired on because he was able to start an old truck. Sixteen Russians formed their own subcontracting crew. Hand work was done by crews organized into station gangs. Pay was good for the times—a man could average $1.15 an hour for excavation work, though less skilled workers received as little as $.50 an hour.

Three workers were killed while the road was being built. One fell sixty feet after he lost his grip on a rope. Another man was killed when he was struck by a rock, and a third fell from the roadway.

On the west side a fairly heavy stand of fir, hemlock, tamarack, cedar, and alder had to be cleared, mostly by hand; the timber was felled, bucked into lengths, and piled by the right-of-way to be used as fuel at the camps or at the two rock crusher plants.

To build a bench on the cliffs for the road to follow, blasting was required. Russell Smith, a project engineer on the road, recalled dangers associated

Bed and board came with the job on the Going-to-the-Sun project. Several camps were constructed along the route to house and feed the workers; some, *top right,* were more substantial than others. Bears, usually blacks but occasionally grizzlies, soon discovered this new food source. Meat was suspended from a pole over a cooktent to keep it from the interlopers. Mrs. Dorothy Price, a cook at one camp, told of a sow named Jean who brought successive sets of twins, Amos and Andy and Nip and Tuck, for handouts. Although the cubs eventually accepted food directly from Mrs. Price, a reprimand from the superintendent put an end to this potentially dangerous activity.

with blasting, especially when black powder was used. Hanging off the cliffs on manila rope, the men would drill holes, into which the powder would be loaded. The highly explosive black powder could be set off unexpectedly by a stray spark. According to Smith, the blasters often worked in stocking feet because of the fear that sparks from the hobnails of their shoes would ignite the powder. Falling rock was a constant hazard, but it was the pre-hardhat era; though some men used war surplus helmets, most simply did not bother.

The limestone from which the road was carved was difficult to drill because it was filled with fissures, which made for bad breaks into large chunks. Two-ton boulders would be rolled downslope by six men with crowbars. In one instance, a Caterpillar tractor attempting to drag a huge boulder went tumbling down the side of a cliff.

Excavation of the 192-foot-long tunnel on the west side did not begin until October 1926. The rest of the road crew had stopped that month, but the tunnel crew persisted until mid-December. Although they lacked only a short distance to break through the west portal, temperatures down to thirty-two below zero delayed them until the following spring.

Snow was a vexing problem. The normal work season was only about two hundred days, and late spring snows had to be cleared before road work could resume. As late as June 19, 1926, enough snow fell to crush several tents at Camp Five. Occasionally, packed snow was blasted to let air circulate in the drifts and speed melting.

The west side was completed in October 1928, a year behind schedule because the contract had been

Before construction could begin each spring, contractors had to clear the roadway of winter snowfall. Steam shovels, *opposite,* were only one type of equipment used to speed the operation. *Above right,* tunnels on each side of Logan Pass had to be cleared of windblown snow and drifts that accumulated at both ends. *Below right,* a stalwart line of prospective contractors got a taste of the snow problem during an inspection trip. Despite the conditions, proper decorum was maintained with hats, coats, and ties.

To get a steam shovel to the site of the east side road construction, workers loaded it onto a pontoon barge and floated it to the head of St. Mary Lake. A small boat, *below,* assisted in the tow. Once the road was partially built, equipment like the road grader, *above left,* was pulled into duty. *Opposite,* workers on upper St. Mary Lake lived in canvas tents, which felt the weight of a winter snowfall sometimes as early as October.

expanded to improve an additional section of road. Attention then turned to the east side. Contracts were let in June 1931, and, as on the west side, the contractors opted to use gas shovels. To solve the access problem, two pontoons were brought by rail to East Glacier Park and trucked to the lower end of Lake St. Mary, where they were tied together and loaded with two shovels, which were barged to the upper end of the lake.

A trail had to be built to get laborers and equipment to the portal of the 408-foot-long tunnel 1½ miles east of Logan Pass. All supplies were hauled from the pass along this trail to a compressor platform. Men packed materials down a 100-foot switchback trail. From that point another 100 feet of nearly vertical ladder led to the bench at the tunnel site. A.V. Emery, engineer in charge, stated that a man in good physical condition could carry a 50-pound box of dynamite down the trail and ladder in a half hour. However, on several occasions men stood at the top of the cliff, "looked down the ladder and turned in their resignation, saying that they could not stand the elevation." Opening the tunnel was a key to finishing other work on the east side. Three shifts toiled around the clock, with the assistance of floodlights at night. At ten p.m. on October 19, 1931, the tunnel was holed through, and final touches were completed by the end of the month. The following fall, contractors proudly completed the east side construction, ahead of schedule. It would be another two years before final gravel surfacing, guardrail installation, and cleanup was finished on the road.

In July 1933, as the glacier lilies were blooming at

July 15, 1933: Going-to-the-Sun Road was officially dedicated during ceremonies at Logan Pass. Hundreds of personal invitations were sent, and thousands of visitors drove to the summit. Under blue skies, a "firefighters' " lunch of chili was served, and numerous dignitaries made speeches of praise. To many, the highlight of the day was the passing of the peace pipe among the

FEEDING BEARS ALONG THE WAY

leaders of the Blackfeet, Kootenai, and Flathead Indian tribes. Park naturalist George Ruhle, *bottom right,* organized the event.

A year later President Franklin D. Roosevelt toured the park and became the first president to travel the Going-to-the-Sun Road. At one point along his route, laborers working on the finishing touches to the highway were allowed to stand and watch the procession. Just before it passed, a crew of CCC boys was ushered in front of the workers to make sure the president received a warm welcome.

MAKES PROBLEM
BEARS ANOTHER DAY

Snow is both a danger and a delight along the Going-to-the-Sun Road. *Top left,* even the first buses over the pass in July 1933 passed towering drifts. Snow removal starts in early spring, but drifts thirty to fifty feet deep make for slow progress. By mid-August nearly all the snow is gone from Logan Pass, but the first fall snowstorm is only weeks away. Avalanches are always a potential threat. *Bottom left,* a watchman stands guard while rescuers search for bodies during the 1953 tragedy. Two men were killed, and another miraculously survived an eight-hour burial after a "sneaker" avalanche swept over them and their equipment.

Logan Pass, the Going-to-the-Sun Road was officially opened to through traffic. Park naturalist George Ruhle was in charge of festivities for the dedication, scheduled for July 15. Special invitations were sent to some four hundred people; various politicians would give speeches; a bronze plaque honoring Stephen Mather would be installed; and a flower show would be set up in the pass. But the highlight of the day would be the smoking of the peace pipe by the Blackfeet, Kootenai, and Flathead Indians, traditional enemies who had hunted in and followed game trails through the mountains.

At noon on July 15 a crowd of four to five thousand people stood as the Blackfeet band played "The Star-Spangled Banner." Following the speeches and unveiling of the plaque, the peace ceremony took place. Representatives of the three tribes examined a bent stick placed at the pass, signifying that the Blackfeet desired peace. The Indians knelt, faced one another, and passed the pipe of peace from right to left, marking an end to years of enmity between them.

The speechmakers praised the road builders and their road and the value of opening the parks to the people. Horace Albright, Stephen Mather's successor as director of the National Park Service, expressed perhaps the most telling sentiment: "Going-to-the-Sun Highway fills the need for quick access to high country to see the glory of Glacier's peaks and crags . . . but parallel roads would add little to the hurrying motorist's enjoyment of the park. . . . Let there be no competition of other roads with the Going-to-the-Sun Highway. It should stand supreme and alone."

Feeding moose. *Opposite*, moss garden near Logan Pass.

Lunch Creek. *Opposite,* St. Mary Lake from Goose Island overlook.

Early morning light from Sun Point. *Opposite,* Going-to-the-Sun Mountain.

Fall scenes: Lower St. Mary Lake and, *opposite,* St. Mary Lake.

Rocky Mountain bighorn sheep. *Opposite*, St. Mary Lake in winter.

Historical photographs were furnished from the following collections: National Park Service, Clarence Bengston, Lawrence Staab, Thain White, and Mel Ruder. The panorama on pages 34 and 35 was photographed by T. J. Hileman.
Appreciation is extended to Clyde Lockwood, Tom Pittenger, Dennis Holden, George Ruhle, and others formerly or now working at Glacier National Park, who generously provided material from park archives and from their memories; to *Hungry Horse News* for the special edition of the *Waterton Glacier Times*, July 15, 1983, marking the fiftieth anniversary of the dedication of Going-to-the-Sun Road.
Oral histories in Glacier National Park collections that were helpful included those given by Eva Beebe, Cora P. Hutchings, Ray Price, Russell Smith, and Ira S. Stinson.

The photographs on the back cover and pages 2, 3, 18, 19, 21, 22, 24, 25, 40, 41, 42, 43, and 45 are by Pat O'Hara © 1984.
The photographs on the front cover, pages 4, 20, 23, 26, 27, 38, 39, 44, 46, 47, and 48 are by Danny On and were furnished by Glacier Natural History Association © 1984.
Project Staff: Design, McQuiston & Daughter; Production, Jana Whitney; Editor, Julie T. Olfe.
Publishing Staff: President, Robert White; Publisher, Eugene G. Schwartz; Office Manager, Marci Wellens.
Typography: Boyer & Brass, Inc., San Diego; Lithography, Paragon Press, Salt Lake City.
Woodlands Press, 853 Camino Del Mar, P.O. Box 728, Del Mar, California 92014